THE NEW MUSIC BUSINESS

FOR INDEPENDENT ARTISTS AND RECORD LABELS

EMMANUEL KENAH, JD.

Copyright © 2019 by Emmanuel Kenah

All rights reserved.

This book or any portion thereof may not be reproduced or used in any manner whatsoever without the express written permission except for the use of brief quotations in a book review. The views expressed here are those of the author.

DISCLAIMER

This book is not intended as a substitute for Legal advice. The reader should consult a Lawyer (Preferably me) in matters relating to their particular situation.

ISBN: 978-0-578-58557-4

©TheStreetLawyer™_2019

DEDICATION

This book is dedicated to:

- **Emma Marie** and all the Black Women in my life (They made me)
- Every Independent Artist and Record Label trying to make sense of the confusion that comes with this industry.
- All the victims of the **MASSIVE GENOCIDE** currently happening in English Speaking Cameroon
- The Houston Public Library, The Lexington Public Library, and The Charleston School of Law Library (where I did most of my research and writing)

A special Shout out to the Artists whose songs I was jamming while doing my research

*Kadijaj - Houston Tx	*Popcaan - St Thomas, Jamaica
*Ei8ht - Houston Tx	* Burna Boy- Nigeria, Africa
* Czure - Nigeria, Africa	*Bobby Buggatti - Houston TX
*Shatta Wale - Ghana, Africa	*Bvocals- Houston, Texas
*Wizkid - Nigeria, Africa	*Yung Al - Houston, Texas
*Victor AD - Nigeria, Africa	*Lilxtenn - Houston, TX
* Quada - Jamaica	*Chronixx - Spanish Town, Jamaica
*Mozzy -Cali, USA	*Cosmic Royalty - Houston, TX
*Kiddo Marv - Miami, Florida	*Jhus- London - UK
*Dave- London, UK	*Mostack- London - UK
*Lil DUrk -Chicago, IL	*Freese Cola - Miami Florida
*Mauii - Lexington, Ky	*Maxo Kream- Houston TX
*Not3 - London, UK	*Jae Prynse - Spanish Town, Jamaica
*Mirror Monk -Miami Fl	*Tae Flo - Houston, TX
*Slim Thug -Houston TX	*Kwesi Arthur- Ghana, Africa
*Zro - Houston TX	*Masicka - Potmore, Jamaica
*Ledge- Nigeria, Africa	*Mavado - Kingston, Jamaica
*J.derobie - Ghana, Africa	*Anokhi the One - Houston Tx
*Erigga - Nigeria, Africa	*Jovi le Monstre - Cameroon, Africa
*Niomie Luvv - Houston Texas	*Kenzolah- Nigeria, West Africa
*Phlowvibes - Houston, TX	*IamDred - Charlotte, NC
*Jah Vinci- Jamaica	* Sam/Sin - Houston, TX
*TaxMan - Dubai, UAE	*Ballers Muzik- Bamenda Cameroon
*Snazzy Shekina- S.A.	*Bella Shmurda- Lagos, Nigeria

PRAISE

"The book answers all the questions many of us indie artists have, and sheds lights on many things we are blind to going into the game. It's given me a shift of confidence as I progress in my own journey as an independent artist."

- KadijaJ (Recording Artist Houston, TX)

Brilliant simplification of all the boiling issues in the Business for artists all over the world.

- Zangchez (Recording Artist, Cameroon, West Africa).

CONTRIBUTIONS

Thanks to my brother, the CEO of NICE GUYS CORPS, Ngang Stephen Ngang, who redesigned the book cover and helped with other design layout.

Thanks to Brittney Stredic of Peculiar Films and Records, who donated her time and skills to the early drafts of the Book cover.

CONTENT

PART ONE

This section examines the changing aspects and business models of the Music industry. It focuses on the revenue sources available to Independent Artists and Record labels including, but not limited to Streaming pay outs from Tidal, YouTube, Spotify etc.; tours; endorsements; and merchandising. This part also focuses on Intellectual Property assets like copyrights, royalties, trademarks and trade secrets. In this part, we are also exposed to Industry lingo.

PART TWO

Independent Artists and Record Labels are Businesses, not just hobbies. This section offers pointers on how artists can properly register and effectively manage themselves as a business. It also examines the various legal entities (Sole Proprietor, Partnership, LLC, Corporations), discussing their advantages and disadvantages.

PART THREE

This section navigates the very important but always neglected topic of Taxes and Bookkeeping for Small businesses. It offers directions on how Indie Artists and Labels (Small Businesses) should file their taxes, when they should file their taxes, and examines the main issues around taxation for small businesses. Indie labels especially, must understand the basics of record keeping for tax purposes and general business management.

PART FOUR

The final part of this book deals with the basics of Contract Law. The music industry is mostly governed by the law of contracts (and Intellectual Property). Record labels extend record deals to up and coming artists, artists recruit producers daily, Companies extend endorsement deals to popping artists, artists recruit management teams and booking agents. There is an unending list of contractual relationships in the Music Business. The Independent Artists and Record Labels, especially in the early stages when they are unable to hire a legal team, are charged with the duties of understanding the basic principles of agreements they make.

PART ONE

THE MUSIC BUSINESS

The music business is experiencing a major shift. Thankfully, it is happening in our lifetime and we are the main proponents of this shift. Everyone has access to the routes once only travelled by the likes of Bob Marley, Prince, Fella Kuti, Michael Jackson, Richard Bona and other greats.

Social media platforms, technology and streaming services have revolutionized the way people listen to and make music. The revenue streams have changed too.

The current music business model is an **access model** while the old music model is a **sales model**. With the sales model, emphasis is on the number of copies sold, thus putting the music in a print format such as a CD or Vinyl serves this purpose. With the access model, emphasis is on making the record available to the public, not necessarily on sales. The advantage of this is that an artist can get paid forever—or, every time someone *accesses* their music. The digital storing format ensures that the song is available anytime, to anyone, anywhere, to access it. The sales model still works but it should be looked on as just one of the revenue sources.

This first part examines the changing aspects of the industry, introduces us to industry lingo, and outlines the "New Music Business Model" along with all its new revenue streams.

CHANGING ASPECTS OF THE MUSIC BUSINESS

Like every other industry in this age, technology has changed the way certain things are done. The old music business model consisted of **selling a whole lot of CDs to upset costs** (Production cost for the music, Manufacturing cost for CD/packaging, Distribution cost, and marketing cost). A label owner who had all four divisions running, controlled a lot of power as they could determine whose music went out to the market. Things have changed, and even though there are still "gate keepers" and "industry plants", they are fewer. Independent artists can now control all four aspects of their music from a MacBook. Industry "old heads" are spending a lot of money fighting streaming platforms, but that has not slowed down the proliferation of successful independent artists who are dependent upon these platforms. Below are some of the aspects that are changing in the industry:

- **DISTRIBUTION**

In the old model, distribution was controlled exclusively by the labels. Label owners had relationships with outlets that served as distribution centers. However, when **Napster** (Not Soulja Boy) came into the game in **1999** with the idea of sharing audio files in MP3 format, they opened the floodgates for what is referred to today as *streaming platforms*. Spotify has over 140 million active users. Other streaming platforms like YouTube, Amazon and iTunes make it easy for an independent artist to make music and distribute without the help of a label.

Distribution outlets still work in the new model, but they only work as one revenue source.

- **COST OF PRODUCTION**

Old recording instruments were mostly heavy and expensive. A lot of people did not have access to recording studios, so the cost of production was very high. Today, songs can be recorded from a laptop in a home studio with no major expenditure. In fact, more songs have been released in this age than ever before. Nobody really needs a label to shine anymore.

- **MARKETING**

It used to be that a band came up with a fire album, the label bought into it, and then forced consumers with the sounds. Labels flooded the market with commercials, CDs, and these songs would get played all day. Consumers became used to it and accepted the songs after a while. *The Breakfast Club, Hot 97*, and other radio stations still do this. They choose which songs and artists to push.

Marketing in this age has become more personalized though. It is no longer about a product, but it is about an experience. Fans hunger for that close interaction. Social media has made this easier for both fans and artists.

- **ROLES**

The music business used to be about roles. There was the production team, the songwriter, the artist (sound recorder), the manager, and the A&R guys. All these units worked together to ensure that everything went smoothly. I did not know how to feel, when I found out that Ed Wheeler and Roger Bowling wrote *"Coward of the County"*. Kenny Rogers only recorded the sound.

Today, the line between these roles is gradually getting wiped out. Most independent artists write, produce and record their projects. They book their shows and manage every aspect of their business. This leads to greater efficiency and reduced costs. *J Cole* and *Big Krit* are examples of artists who are involved in almost every aspect of their projects.

Independent artists however, should seek assistance with the technical aspects of their business. Having a lawyer and tax specialist to run stuff by is a great benefit.

STREAMING PLATFORMS AND SELLING YOUR MUSIC ONLINE.

For independent artists in the digital age, the aim should be to commercialize your craft by increasing your following on social media and streaming platforms. A great internet campaign can raise revenue which you would otherwise not realize from a typical record deal. People get rich daily by uploading viral content on YouTube and iTunes. There are many streaming services currently being used in the industry. Artists may need to make certain considerations before choosing one streaming service over the other, to upload their music.

Different streaming services pay different amounts per play. They also have different market shares, meaning that even though a streaming service is paying the highest, you might not make the most money from them because they control a very small section of the market.

Last year alone, the combined income realized by Universal, Sony, and Warner Music from streaming services like *Spotify*, *iTunes* and *YouTube* came up to a whopping $14.2 **million a day.**

Live music sales are estimated to go from the current **7.5 billion to 9.2 billion in 2021. Last year Vinyl sales went** up by 26%. What does this mean to the independent artist and record label? In one simple sentence, "there is enough Benjamins to go around."

Independent artists and record labels should create artists profiles with the top streaming services. There are services that can help you distribute your music to these platforms and collect the royalties on your behalf; **DistroKid and TuneCore** amongst other companies can help distribute your music for a once a year flat fee.

Below are the top players/payers in the streaming business:

STREAMING PLATFORMS/SERVICES	PAY PER PLAY	TOTAL FOR 100k PLAYS	MARKET SHARE
• SPOTIFY	$0.0038	$380	51.51%
• ITUNES	0.00793	$793	21.02%
• PANDORA	$0.00134	$134	7.86%.
• GOOGLE	$0.0063	$630	4.0%
• AMAZON	$0.0074	$740	3.80%
• DEEZER	$0.0056	$560	3.24%
• TIDAL	$0.0110	$110	1.76%
• RHAPSODY/NAPSTER	$0.01682	$1,682	1.75%
• YOUTUBE	$0.00074	$74	8.4%
• XBOX MUSIC	$0.02730	$2,730	0.65%

Most of these platforms pay a fixed amount per play. The amounts may seem insignificant, but they can add up especially if you are registered with more than one. It is recommended to register with the top ten streaming platforms, since this is the main revenue source in the new music business. These numbers are estimates, as several other factors go into the streaming payouts including country where it's being played, and personal arrangements with particular streaming platforms.

Driving your art to where you **can have a minimum of 100,000 plays on various platforms**, should be one of the early goals of any artist looking to make a living out of the music business. This is a very achievable goal for any artist or record label constantly working on their craft. It should take about 6 months of continuous work to get to a 100k views. California rapper Mozzy said something like... we must do this for the GAIN and not only for the FAME. The internet chooses what it chooses; make sure they choose your work!

Below are a few clarifications from the table above:

- **Streams Vs Plays**

Streaming refers to the ability to listen to an audio or watch a movie without downloading it. You can stream a video from YouTube, Netflix, or other sources.

Plays, on the other hand, is just the number of times listeners get to hear your song. For it to count as a "play" for the purpose of earning money, it must run for the first 30 seconds at least. I know you are a rebel (invisible wink); beat the system, but not like this.

- **Deezer**

A lot of artists and record labels are familiar with the nine other streaming platforms, but Deezer is lesser known. This is a French-based streaming platform which is very popular in Eastern and Western Europe. Putting your music on a platform like this gives you exposure to new fans in different countries. Deezer is doing exceedingly good in Europe and control a small percentage of the American Market. There are independent artists who are celebrities in other countries and have no idea.

- **Market Share Consideration**

While the payout rate (POR) is one of the greatest considerations in determining where to hosts your music, we must consider the market share and market access offered by other platforms that pay less. The table takes all this in to consideration. However, everybody should do their research and pick accordingly. There are many more streaming platforms, but these ten platforms accounts for about 96% of the total market.

- **Tidal**

Apart from Tidal having one of the best pay out rates, this streaming service has some of its users as partners. Even though the check might not be that much, their pay out rates are high. It is important to drive traffic towards your tidal account. I do not know why everybody does not have a Tidal account. If we are to take back the "culture", Tidal will be vital in this process. Let's make Tidal Great!

Hold Up! Before we go too far, let us differentiate between two important concepts that will guide the rest of our discussions: **Royalties and Licenses**

ROYALTIES VS LICENSES

These are both great ways to generate income as an artist, but they have some slide differences which are important to examine.

Royalties is the money that an artist makes when their music is played in public places (**Performance royalties**) or his original recordings are duplicated (**Mechanical royalties**) by a label. More on how to collect your royalties in subsequent pages.

Licenses operate almost the same. This is the permission that an artist gives to any other person to use their composition. Once an artist puts their music out to the public, they cannot stop people from using it even though they own it. This permission to use another's music is what is called a license. Licenses could be compulsory or discretionary. **Compulsory Licenses** have their rates set by the copyright act, while **discretionary licenses** do not have any fix rates but could be negotiable between the user and owner.

OTHER SOURCES OF REVENUE

The popularization of the Internet has offered independent artists and record labels tremendous opportunities that did not exist ten years ago. However, there are certain aspects from the old Music Model (**sales model**) that still work today. Below is a list of other revenue sources in the Music Business. They all apply differently to different artists, so choose those that work best for you.

- **Endorsement deals:** There is the typical endorsement deal where Sprite, for example, gives J Cole some money to promote their products. Most Independent Artists do not have the connections to earn these huge deals. It is important for independent artists to approach local businesses, club owners, mom and pop shops with proposals about marketing their products to the independent artist's fan base. The compensation **must not** be financial. An artist may promote another's business in exchange for a free venue or free merchandise.

- **Tours/Merchandise/Shows**: Keeping up with your fan base is important in the new music business. Fans come from different areas of the country or city. It is important to take your show to your fans once you have a body of work. It does not matter if they are 10 or 1000, take the show on the road and during those shows, make contacts, network and most importantly, sell merchandise (T-shirts, hats, etc.). Kendrick Lamar still has and often recounts fun memories from when he used to perform to a ten-man audience.

• **CD Sales:** While most of your distribution will be focused online, it is important to have hard copies. Some people still like their CDs. CDs are easy to carry and your supporters can buy a CD for $5. The cost of production of a CD is about 80cents, and if sold for $5, an artist is making more than a 200% profit. Dropping your CDs in Barber shops, local grocery shops, and other brick and mortar stores will ease your distribution. Give the shops a dollar for every CD they sell so it motivates them to sell it.

• **Features and Collaborations:** If an artist is really popping, a way to make money is by charging other artists for features. If they want the sauce, they must pay for the sauce (but remember not to get lost in the sauce). Some collaborations will be free, but for those who can afford, put a price on it. I was going through IG last year, and my boy **Mirror Monk** (Florida Rapper) mentioned he made $9000 in a week off features alone. While you will not start off with this amount, when you get the sauce like him, you can charge whatever you think your value is.

- **Government Grants:** States, cities and councils have grants dedicated to encouraging certain activities including but not limited to creative acts, cultural acts, and small businesses. Do your research and apply for those grants. Check your local council website for information on any partnerships or events that strive to invest in independent artists and the arts.

- **Crowdfunding/ External Help:** There exist several online platforms to help people raise money from the public. This has tax implications; you should consult with an attorney. **GoFundMe** is an example of this.

Another great way is by getting your "money-friends", family members and supporters to finance your projects. If they talk the talk, make them walk the walk.

- **Commercializing your Intellectual Property:** Apart from your physical assets, you have intangible assets collectively called **intellectual property**. They include trademarks, copyrights, and in rare cases patents. This will be the subject of the next part of this chapter.

INTELLECTUAL PROPERTY

There are two **main** branches of law that govern the music business: **Contract Law** and **Intellectual Property Law**. The basics of Contract law will be examined in Part 4 of this book.

What is Intellectual Property Law?

An artist can have physical assets as well as non-physical assets. These physical assets include real property (e.g. land, houses) and tangible property (e.g. Cars, clothes).

Artists also own **non-physical assets which include ideas, creative works and design concepts.** The laws governing the ownership of these ideas, creative works, and design concepts is what is collectively referred to as Intellectual Property Law.

Intellectual Property is anything created by the human intellect that the law will protect and give **exclusive use** to the creator for a fixed period. When this right is protected, an artist can make money off these non-physical assets (royalties).

So, when an artist records a song, a producer makes a beat, a writer pens a book or script; they all create intellectual property (Yes, put on your hero cape; you are a creator!).

Securing their rights in this intellectual property created, is what guarantees that they are *paid in full* (get it?) for their work.

Intellectual Property Rights (IPR)

IPRs give the creator of the intellectual property, the exclusive right to use or sell their idea or work for a specified period. Where there are rights, the law offers protections. There are four main types of Intellectual Property Protections: **Patents, Trade Secrets, Copyrights, and Trademarks.**

For an independent artist, the focus should be on the Copyrights and Trademarks.

- **Copyrights**

Copyrights protect original works of the brain like **literary works, music, dramatic works, choreographic works, sculptural, pictorial, graphic works, sound recordings, artistic works, architectural works, and computer software.**

Works that are "still in the head" do not qualify for copyright protection. To enjoy this protection, **the words must be affixed to a tangible medium of expression** like writing words on a piece of paper or recording music onto a computer system.

Copyrights exist from the moment the ideas are affixed to a tangible medium, but an artist gets extra protection (**statutory damages, attorney fees and court cost**) if they formally register their work.

Artists can register their work in the US, by filling an online form and submitting a copy of their work on the **US Copyright Office Website**. It costs **$35 per filing**.

Copyrights are non-renewable and last the lifetime of the author plus 70years. copyright protection gives the holder an exclusive right to modify, distribute, perform, create, display, copy and license the work.

- **Trademarks™ or Servicemarks℠**

Trademarks or Servicemarks are **words, phrases, symbols, or designs that distinguish the products (trademarks) or services (service marks)** of one business from its competitors. *The Adidas three bands, Dj Khaled's "We the Best", or the name TIDAL are all examples of symbols, phrases, or words respectively that can be trademarked. A logo is another example of a trademark.*

Rights in a mark are acquired by use but an artist can get extra protection (**statutory damages, attorney fees and court cost**) if they formally register their work.

Before registering a trademark, artists should **search state and federal database** to ensure that there is nobody using a similar mark for the same products.

Trademarks can be registered in the US through the **US Patents and Trademark Office website**. **The cost ranges from $250-$400** for a standard Trade or Service mark.

Using the ™ sign on your product has no legal significance, except that it gives notice to your competitors that you intend to use the mark or have filed for a registration on that mark. Once approved, artists can begin using the ® symbol behind their mark.

These processes are complicated especially for beginners, please consult with an attorney for assistance with this, better still, call me.

Making Money from Your Intellectual Property

In the new music industry, as previously noted, streaming payouts are a major way to make money. We have also examined other sources of revenue in the industry, but a major source we have left untouched this far **are the royalties generated from the licensing of copyrighted songs.**

Once an artist copyrights a song, it gives them an exclusive right over the song, and if others want to use/sample this song, they will **have to pay a licensing fee or in other words, royalties.** The license permits an individual who is not the owner of the copyrighted or trademarked material, to legally use it.

To understand how these payments are made to musicians, we must distinguish between the two types of musicians- **songwriters and performing artists**. While Songwriters hold the rights to the words and melody in a song, performing artists hold the right to a particular recording, also referred to as the master recording. **Songwriters earn Mechanical royalties**, while **performing Artists earn Performance Royalties.**

For the independent artists who write, produce, and record their songs, they own both the performance and mechanical rights. Artists should register with **the separate** entities in charge of collecting and distributing these royalties.

- **Performance Royalties**

A fee is paid when music is performed publicly. Private enjoyment of music will not result in the payment of this fee, mostly because for a person to play music on their phone or own a cd, they likely have bought it already. However, when music **is played in restaurants, on the radio, or over streaming platforms like Spotify or Pandora, the recording artist earns royalties.**

Those who play others Music in their businesses or on the internet radio, owe the artist a fee.

Performance Rights Organizations are charged with collecting these fees and distributing them to the artists. In **the US, the main PROs are BMI, ASCAP, and SESAC.**

Artists need to register with only one of these PROs.

- **Mechanical Royalties (MR)**

A **song writer** earns mechanical royalties anytime their songs are **reproduced, retransmitted, or streamed on demand**. Independent Artists own their Masters (original work) and are entitled to this kind of royalty. However, when an artist signs a record deal, the label owns rights to these Masters. This could be negotiated depending on how good of an artist you are or how good of a lawyer you have (call me).

Chris Brown, signed to RCA, recently renegotiated his deal in which he was given the rights to all his Masters. This makes him the youngest artist to own his Masters.

The current Mechanical Royalty payout rate is fixed at about **9 cents for every CD sold**. If 10,000 CDs are printed, then the songwriter makes 0.9 multiplied by 10,000 copies, and that gives us $9000 just for mechanical royalties.

For major publishers, this is collected by the **Harry Fox Agency** which is a government agency charged with this function. Apart from registering with a PRO, artists should register with the Harry Fox Agency on their website.

These are the two major types of royalties in the music business, but **Sync royalties** and **Printed Music Royalties also exist**.

Sync Royalties are paid when a song is combined with an **audio-visual production** e.g. TV Shows, movies, video games and smartphone apps. Printed Music Royalty is paid when an artist's music is **printed on a sheet or the lyrics are published in print form**.

BEAT LICENSING

In earlier pages, we encountered the term licensing in connection with recordings. **Here we are examining licensing from a producer/beat maker standpoint.** To record any heat song, the process begins with having a heat beat (for most people). Most independent artists have taught themselves the art of beat creation/making. **Beat making and ghost writing** are very important revenue streams in this new music business. As a newcomer in to the industry, it is difficult to know what your beats are worth or how to get paid from your original creation. When my friend and rising vocalist, Brittney Balma tried to get a beat online and the producer wanted to keep 50% of all earnings, I thought there was some foul game. Upon research, I found that he was well within his rights. If I was confused about this, I figured, a few more people were to. So, I decided to include this section for the culture.

With respect to beat making, **licensing is an arrangement where one party (the licensor/beatmaker) gives the other party (licensee/ artist) the right to use an original beat.** This license is usually given, in exchange for a fee. The amount fluctuates, depending on the kind of license and other factors. A beat license may either be **exclusive** or **non-exclusive.**

- **Non-Exclusive Beat Licensing**

When a producer of a beat gives you a non-exclusive license, it means he gives you **specific but limited rights** to use his beat. You can record on the beat, but the producer still retains the copyright ownership in the beat and until you fully pay for the beat, the producer has the right to sell it to whomever he chooses.

In trying to copyright a song with a nonexclusive beat license, you can copyright your lyrics as a **derivative work of the original track**. With a nonexclusive license, you do not have any publishing rights and so **cannot** make money from the song. A typical example is the sample beats producers have on their websites.

- **Exclusive Beat Licensing**

With an exclusive license, the producer gives the artists **complete rights** to the song. The artists can exploit the masters in the song anywhere and anyhow they like. Once an artist's purchases the exclusive rights to a beat, the **producer can no longer** sell it to any other person.

Some producers have you pay a minimum upfront cost for a beat and negotiate the publishing rights. A **50/50 split** between producer and artist on the revenue from a song is the going industry standard but depending on the leverage the artists possess; this can be negotiated.

Other producers prefer a one-time settlement. They tax you a higher onetime payment and relinquish all their interest in the song, including publishing rights.

TheStreetLawyer's TidBit

- Independent Artists at the start of their career need to work on getting a good fan base. They do not need to drop big money in trying to own exclusive beats. A good way to go about the early stages is to make mixtapes and covers. These are inexpensive but put you in the mix. Once you get people ready to buy your music, then you can invest in exclusive beats and recoup this money from song and merchandize sales.

- Indie artists should try to keep production within the crew. Rather than sharing your royalties with strangers, build your team and negotiate fair rates with them

- Producers should always have a split agreement with artists they believe in. This will entail taking a small amount from the artist upfront and getting a huge cut (up to 50% of revenue) once the song does good.

What is a split sheet?
A split sheet is a document that **denotes every party's contribution to a song and the percentage of that contribution.** It is standard industry practice to have an agreement with all the names of the various contributors and their roles in a project.

If Beatsbyallday produces a beat, and Lil Woss records on the beat; the typical split-sheet will show Beatsbyallday as the producer, and Lil Woss as the artist. It will also show that Beatsbyallday is entitled to 50% of the revenue from the song (after cost) and Lil Woss is entitled to the other half.

In another scenario, it may be that five different artists collaborate on a song, the split sheet will have to reflect this and their levels of contribution. If an artist came up with the hook and that's the most played part of the song, it only makes sense that in negotiating, they are given a higher percentage than somebody who just uttered one line.

A split shit is **how people get paid for collaborations** and it is advisable to create and **sign one before publishing** the song. With a split sheet in place, the royalties will be divided by the performing rights organization to reflect the percentages therein.

PART ONE BONUS MATERIAL
Music Business Checklist for Independent Artists and Record Labels

I am committed to assisting you bring your vision to reality. Below are the steps required to get your music venture up and running. This list will help you evaluate where you stand and where you are headed as a business. This is an overview of the general process. Be sure to contact me with questions.

1. **Choose and Register Legal Structure**

You have 4 choices

    a) **Sole Proprietorship**

    b) **Partnership**

    c) **Limited Liability Company**

    d) **Corporation or S-Corporation**

2. **Register a domain name**

In today's economic and entrepreneurial ecosystem, securing an online domain name for your business is a must.

It helps if the domain name matches your artist name. This is also one of your intellectual property assets that must be trademarked.

.com names are usually more "official looking" and are hardly free. They are however very affordable.

3. **Register Social Media handles**

It is important to have **Facebook, Instagram, Snap Chat, Twitter** etc. It encourages engagement with your target audience and it's an easy way to get direct feedback.

4. **Register your Copyrights**

In the US, as soon as you affix your ideas to a medium (electronic or physical) your written works or sound recordings are protected. To get added legal rights, you must register your original writings and sound recordings (Songs, poetry, movie scripts etc.) with the **US Copyright Office**. It is easier to process electronic registrations

5. **Register trademarks for your Name and Logo**

Names can be an artist's biggest asset as it can promote merchandise, goodwill, and endorsements. It is important to protect these assets with the **US Patents and Trademark Office**.

6. **Establish a Written Contract between Partners**

If you are going to operate with other partners (Producers, Directors, Sound Engineers, etc.), it is important that you have a contract that covers who will contribute what, and how royalties are going to be split **(Split agreement)**. If you register as an LLC, this can be done on the **Operating Agreement**.

7. **Choose a Songwriting or Performance Rights Organization (PRO)**

Buying a song on iTunes entitles you to private enjoyment of the song. Businesses play music all the time. These songs are incidental to their purpose (Dinners, nightclubs etc.) and are entitled to pay a fee when they use your copyrighted music in their venues. PRO help you collect these royalties. **ASACP,**

BMI and **SESAC** all PROs in the US and you need to register only with one since they all do the same thing.

8. **Register with Harry Fox Agency**

While the PROs are charged with collecting your Performance Rights royalties, the U.S. government has entrusted the **Harry Fox Agency**, to collect and distribute **Mechanical Royalties**. These are royalties that **come from the reproduction of copyrighted works**. Unlike PRR, Mechanical Royalties are 100% of the entitlement to the songwriter. Let's say you drop a hot single and a distribution agency approaches you to "move" the song. You are entitled to **9.1cents** (Statutory rate) for every copy reproduced. This could be huge, if the single makes crazy numbers.

9. **Register with SoundExchange**

Those who perform on a sound recording or owned masters to the sound recording, are entitled to royalties from anyone who streams the track digitally. Sound Exchange is charged by the US government with the responsibility to distribute these royalties. Did I mention it's free to register?

10. **Set Up Distribution Channels**

In today's climate, artists must focus on physical and digital distribution. There exist a lot of platforms to make your music available to consumers.

Registering with **CDbaby** will help you in the distribution of your CDs, and vinyl.

Registering with organizations like **distroKid, TuneCore**, The Orchid, or similar companies will help make your music available for purchase on streaming services such as **iTunes, Amazon, Spotify, Deezer, Tidal** etc.

11. Embed Metadata about each track on to the Digital File

Metadata is the information about the track which will include **name of artist, name of track, label name, album** etc. This helps in the collection process of your royalties. Most mastering software come with these services.

12. Build A Heavy Web Presence

Through your website and social media, you **can sell your music, promote your platform, sell merchandise, share news, tour dates and updates**. Use this for the right reasons.

13. Secure Insurance

You are a business, man! By all means, get insurance. The two most important are **health and equipment insurance**. They are very cheap and affordable options. Do your research!

14. Build A Team

It is important to have a solid team around you. A great team ensures that more content can be produced and distributed within a short period of time. It means you will have to pay for some services. It is important to get somebody to handle **social media, bookings, video, licensing, accounting, and legal stuff**. Surround yourself with winners.

15. Keep Refining your Product

To become an expert in anything, we must put in at least 10,000 practice hours. Once credits are calculated in school to reach 10,000, a PHD is awarded. Your 10,000 practice hours will be calculated from how much time you spend in the studio WORKING.

16. Stay Humble and Network

My final advice is to stay humble and stay in the mix. The Music Business in particular is a relationship-based business. Make sure you don't burn bridges, avoid the fake, and keep working.

TheStreetLawyer's TidBit

- Put your Music on at least **six streaming platforms** (Spotify, Tidal, YouTube, iTunes, Deezer, Sound Cloud).

- Get social media popping

- Use **YouTube to put up your visuals** and other content

- CD Baby Pro registers your songs with Performing Rights Organizations and collection societies in the US and abroad for the collection of publishing royalties.

- Performance Royalties: ASCAP, BMI, SESAC

- Mechanical Royalties: Harry Fox, Music Reports

Apart from online streams, a heavy focus should be put on merchandise sales and organizing performances in local bars and shops, to promote your music. Independent artists can always seek endorsements from local business in exchange for promotions. Most independent artists should already have a great following. They can leverage to get financial support from local business owners based on their following

PART TWO

THE INDEPENDENT ARTIST AS A BUSINESS

The first time I heard about an artist being a business, I was captured instantly. This was in 2005, before slaves had a choice; years before the word "lit" even existed. On *Diamonds from Sierra Leone*, one of the tracks from Kanye's well acclaimed "Late Registration" which featured Tidal boss, Jay Z, flowing in typical HOV style:

"I do this in my sleep

I sold kilos of coke, I'm guessin' I can sell CD's

I'm not a businessman; I'm a business, man!

Let me handle my business, damn!"

What HOV tried to tell the rest of the world in 2005—and they did not listen—is the same message this book has for independent artists and record labels today. If we look at HOV's journey since 2005, it has been phenomenal to say the least. Maybe it's time we start listening to that man more closely. Jay for Pres!

Indie artists and labels must start looking at themselves as a business, if they want to reap all the benefits of their craft.

Part two of this book gives directions on **how to effectively organize, register and hold yourself out as a small business.**

A. HOW TO REGISTER YOUR BUSINESS

Small businesses always ask the question, "How do I get registered?" Registering a business is not an act but a process. This process depends on the type of business and the state in which you are trying to register the business. For new businesses, this process involves:

- Registering with the IRS
- Registering Business as a Legal Entity
- Registering Company/Trade name
- Registering for Business licenses and permits.

There is no particular order, but it is advisable to register your business in this order for easy follow up. Examine these steps below:

- **Registering with IRS**

The IRS issues businesses a free **Employee Identification Number (EIN),** also known as a Tax ID. This number serves as the business' social security number and is needed to file taxes or carry any financial transaction on behalf of company.

This is necessary only for **Corporations, LLCs and Partnerships**, as Sole Proprietors can still use their SSN in place of a Tax ID.

You will need this number to make your quarterly estimated tax payments.

- **Registering Business as Legal Entity**

Not all businesses need to be registered. Sole Proprietors and Partnerships can skip this step, but **LLCs and Corporations must register with the Secretary of State** within the county where they are located or operate. This is done by filing the **Articles of Incorporation** and for most states, a registered agent must be chosen. The registered agent receives all service process on behalf of the Company.

- **Registering Company/Trade Name**

A business name is a major asset. It helps set the business apart from other businesses. Before registering your business as a legal entity, **you must make sure your name is available**, if it is, then you can apply for a trade or service mark with the United States Patent and Trademark Office.

If you are a limited liability company or Corporation, you must denote your name as such (LLC, and Inc. respectively). It is easier to use the name without the LLC for some products, but without "deceiving" the consumer, it is advisable to apply for a DBA (Assumed Business Name/ Doing Business As) with your state government. For example, **Wizkid's** business is registered as **Stew LLC**, but he has trademarked "Stew" and wants to use it as the business name. All he must do is go to his county courthouse and apply for an assumed business name, then he can start using Stew instead of Stew LLC.

- **Apply for Business Licenses and Permits**

Most businesses do not require any particular permit to start functioning in certain states. This varies by business and by state, so be sure to contact your **Small Business Administration (SBA)** for your state and be advised of which licenses you need.

Most retail and small businesses collect sales taxes from their customers. Business owner should apply for **a Sales Tax Permit from the State Revenue Office/State Comptroller.**

To run a business, the **most essential thing is to have a product or an idea.** Even though this is the most important thing, it is just the FIRST step to properly running your business. A business must be registered with the relevant state, county and federal authorities.

Registering with these authorities is advantageous as it ensures that:

*there is limitation of liability. For some business types, registration limits the liability of partners. Where the business suffers a loss the liability of partners is limited only to company assets and not their personal assets.

*a company can open a bank account and build company credit. Most entrepreneurs have messed up their personal credit on other prior unsuccessful ventures. You must miss a few to hit the right one! Registering a business is a great way to build business credit which could help with small business cash flow. Business bank accounts have flexibility that personal accounts do not have.

*you enjoy supplier discounts. Showing that you are a registered business and having a **Sales Tax Permit** will lead to wholesale suppliers giving goods at wholesale prices and without the taxes.

*a business has credibility and exposure. It gives clients the ease to patronize your business knowing that you are registered with the authorities.

*the business benefits from all state and federal allocations reserved for the support of businesses

B. CHOICE OF LEGAL ENTITY

After looking at the advantages of registering your business entity and going through the process of getting established; one important question that remains is with regards to the choice of entity.

Businesses will have to make this decision very early. However, it is not a permanent decision; **the structure can be changed** to accommodate any present situation.

There are four broad business entity choices:

- Sole proprietor
- Partnership
- Limited Liability Company
- Corporations (S and C-Corps)

Each entity choice has different **implications on taxes, permits, schedules and deadlines.**

- **Sole Proprietor**

If no other entity is noted, this is the default entity. **Sole Proprietor is a one-man business.** The business and the owner are so intertwined they are one. Every time the business takes a loss, it counts as personal debt and every time the business makes profits, it counts as personal income. It

does not have to be registered, and the owner's SSN can be used for financial transactions.

To **open a business account as a sole proprietor, take your SSN and ID** to the county courthouse and apply for an **Assumed Business Name (DBA)**. This is the only additional document you need to open a business bank account when you are a sole proprietor.

- **Partnership**

Partnerships have been given all kinds of names in business. A typical partnership consists **of two or more people joining resources and running a business.** One partner is fully responsible for the actions of the other partner. Regardless of who does more work, the profits are shared equally.

To deal with this presumed inequality, partners need to establish a **partnership agreement at the beginning of their partnership,** which should specify what happens in case of dissolution or where one person decides to quit. It should clearly indicate each partner's responsibilities and contribution to the business

This agreement has the effect of **limiting one partner's liability for the wrongful acts** of the other partner.

- Corporations

We **are not going to have much** of a discussion about this entity type because small businesses hardly ever operate as such. For general information and for those ambitious readers who are headed down this path, we will discuss the basics.

With most corporations, **we let other people invest in the company or we can publicly raise money**. It must be in line with SEC (Security and Exchange Commission) rules.

The SEC is the federal agency entrusted with the duty of **protecting investors, maintaining fairness and order in the securities market.**

There are two types of Corporations denoted by their chapters in the tax code **(S-Corps and C-Corps).**

The most important thing here is the **liability shield between personal assets and company assets**.

- Limited Liability Company (LLC)

This is the most recent entity type. This only became popular in the US in the early 2000s. **It mimics some properties of the partnership and others from corporations.**

With an LLC, the members report their personal tax returns but enjoy the protection of a corporation with their assets.

There are **single member LLCs** which give sole proprietors corporate protection **and multi member LLCs**. An **Operating Agreement** discussing capital contribution, rights and duties, and other arrangements is a very essential document in a multi-member LLC.

LLCs can be **Member-managed** or **Manager-managed**.

Table: Below is a table distinguishing the main features of these business entities.

	SOLE PROPRIETOR	PARTNERSHIP	LLC
Legal Status	Same as owner	Different from Owner	Different from Owner
Owner Liability	Unlimited liability	**General Partner:** Unlimited liability **Limited Partner:** Limited liability	Limited liability to investment except for personal services
Management	Managed by owner	Managed by Partners	Manager or Member managed
Self-Employment Tax	Yes	Yes for Gen Partner, No for Ltd Partner	Depends on entity choice for tax purposes
Formation	Nothing needs to be done	Nothing, but Partnership Agreement is strongly recommended	File Articles of Formation with the Secretary of State
Advantages	-Flexibility in decision making -	-Possibility to raise more capital. -Assistance in decision making and running business.	-Limits liability of owner -Taxed as individuals but protected as Corp. -Formal Structure
Disadvantages	-Bears all losses -No Limited Liability -No Formal Structure	-One partner can ruin the business. -no formal Structure Unlimited liability	-Slow decision-making process in Multi-member LLCs.

©TheStreetLawyerTM_2019

 **TheStreetLawyer's TidBit**

It is best to **register as an LLC**. This is the most flexible business structure and offers Corporate Liability Protection to its member(s) while taxing them as sole proprietors or partners. **LLCs are a combination of the best aspects** of a partnerships, sole proprietorships and corporations.

CONGRATULATIONS if you made it to this point. It can sometimes be overwhelming to start and run a business, but I have realized, as in most things, it is best to break it down into tiny chunks, to create action plans and, set goals.

I have broken down these tasks into manageable chunks. Follow the Checklist below and you should be on your way to starting your very own business. (You can reap off this page and carry with you)

PART TWO BONUS MATERIAL

Small Business Startup Checklist

I am committed to assisting you bring your vision to reality. Below are the steps required to form your business and get it moving. This list will help you evaluate where you stand and where you are headed as a business. This is an overview of the general process, be sure to contact me with questions.

1. **Pick a Name**

Search Federal, State and other internet resources to make sure the name is not taken.

2. **Choose and Register Legal Structure**

You have 4 choices

- Sole Proprietorship
- Partnership
- Limited Liability Company
- Corporation or S-Corporation

3. **Register a domain name**

In today's economic and entrepreneurial ecosystem, securing an online domain name for your business is a must.

It helps if the domain name matches the business name. This is also one of your intellectual property assets. .com names are usually more "official looking" and are hardly free. They are however very affordable.

4. Write a Business Plan

It helps to have your idea written on paper, even if it is not the complete plan or does not follow the format of a typical business plan. A mission statement will work just as good here.

5. Get Website Running

You might not have your product ready yet, but it is important to have a website for credibility. Put up your company and product information to update early visitors on your progress. They are going to serve as your base crowd when you launch.

6. Register Social Media Profiles

Even if you intend to run a strictly brick and mortar store, it is important to have Facebook, Instagram, Snap Chat, Twitter etc. It encourages engagement with your target audience and it's an easy way to get untainted feedback.

7. Secure your Employer Identification Number (EIN)/Tax ID

You will need an **Employer Identification Number** (EIN) to open a bank account or access payroll. This will serve as your tax identification number for all interactions with the IRS.

8. Open a Business Bank Account

It is important to separate business funds from personal funds. A business bank account helps you build business credit. You can always obtain a loan from the bank to help with expansion or other projects. Be sure to check interest rates before accepting loans though.

9. Apply for Licenses and Permits

Depending on your business, you may require federal permits, state licenses, or city permits. If you sell physical products within a state, you may need to secure a sale tax permit.

10. **Determine whether you are going to have employees or independent contractors.**

You will have to obtain Workers Compensation Insurance or Unemployment Insurance if you have employees.

11. **Establish your bookkeeping methods**

Apps such as QuickBooks can help you organize your paperwork. Bookkeeping helps you keep up with cash flow and expense, account receivables and account payables.

12. **Secure Corporate paperwork**

Setup your accounting and record-keeping system and learn about the specific taxes your new company is responsible for paying. Keep all paperwork for at least 3 years.

13. **Brand your Business**

This can be done effectively through promotional materials and merchandise. Designing a professional logo can drive more business.

14. List all your Assets and Protect them

List all business assets and secure them with insurance. Also, list intellectual property assets and protect them. Trademark all names and logos, copyright all written material and sound recordings for your protection.

15. Let People Know

You are completely set up at this point. Develop a marketing plan and reach out to your ideal customers. Social Media can be a great tool.

16. Refine your Sales Pitch

Every business owner needs to be able to highlight their products and services to investors, customers and partners. A strong 90-seconds pitch is a great intro point.

 **TheStreetLawyer's TidBit**

Starting out in any business, be it technology or music, we must constantly evaluate how to drive growth. As soon as we start working, it is easy to become overwhelmed because building a business is an enormous task. Below is a compilation of things we can do to make sure we are growing the business even if our early returns do not seem to say the same:

- Focus on Your **Mission Statement**

Every business should have a five-line Mission statement that explains what exactly the business is about. If you are opening a business for charitable reasons, **your goals will be different** from a person opening it strictly for profit maximization.

- The **fewer products you offer**, the better

Specialization results in efficiency. If you are an artist, focus on a **specific genre and become an expert at it**. If you own a clothing or shoe line, reduce the number of products offered so you can efficiently manage and make sure your products are the best.

- Do not let **Social Media Get to You**

It is important to use Social media, but you must go for quality over quantity. You **might have ten followers who spend $1,000** on your business every month and another person might have a million followers and makes no revenue from them. Stay on top of the trends but do not get too engaged with social media. It's distracting!

- Make **PROFIT**

Even if your main aim is not to maximize profit, we have to **meet our bottom line** in order to achieve our humanitarian goals. For the independent artist, **we have to EAT**. It is important for your peace of mind too.

Examples/Explanation and Lessons

Most of the concepts covered in the earlier pages of this book are new and a little bit difficult to understand. I have chosen throughout this book, certain events, stories and people whose grind could better help us understand what we must be doing as independent artists. Everybody is unique, there are a thousand different ways to do the same thing but examining history could help us avoid certain errors and help us know where to focus most of our energies and often limited resources.

- **The Percy Miller Story (Master P)**

Ice Cube called Master P "one of the best businessmen I've ever run across," and record executive Tony Draper declared him "a young successful black C.E.O. who has the intelligence to take the rap business to the next level."

Master P was an Independent Artist before the term existed. He figured something about the game that a lot of artists are yet to discover. It will do this book no justice to talk about independent artists without mentioning the patron saint of all independent artists. When he was still struggling as an artist in the early 90's, Master P was offered a One-million-dollar record deal by Jimmy Iovine of Interscope Records. He turned that deal down because he realized that most artist at the time were making just about 10% of their royalties.

Master P enrolled as a freshman in the University of Houston where he had a basketball scholarship. He dropped out after the first semester and went in to Merrit Junior College in Oakland California where he studied business for two years. It was during this period that his grandfather passed away and he was awarded $10,000 as settlement for a malpractice lawsuit surrounding the death. It was with this money that Master P opened his first record store- No Limits Records. He used this record store to scope the trends within the hip-hop industry and noticed a shortage in "gangster rap". Seeing this, he jumped in that market and dropped a couple of albums. When these albums did not do well, he moved his label and store back to New Orleans where he enjoyed major success on his next two projects (*The Ghetto is trying to Kill me* and *99 ways to Die*). Because he did not have a record deal, Master P promoted the albums through word of mouth and sold through local music stores. There was no streaming at the time, and he managed to sell about 250,000 copies.

Seeing what he could accomplish independently, Master P became hungry for more success. If a label was willing to give him a million dollars, he reasoned he was worth five times that. Master P did his research and found that Michael Jackson, at the time, had the best deal in the business in which he kept 80% of his royalties and the label kept 20%. Bent on having the same deal, Master P reached out to Michael Jackson's lawyer who charged him $25,000 to make it happen. Master P, understanding that you had to spend money to make money, quickly paid the lawyer who negotiated a **DISTRIBUTION DEAL** between No Limit Records and Priority Records. According to the fine print, and true to his wishes, an 80/20 deal was negotiated in which Master P kept all his Masters (Mechanical Royalties) plus 80% of his Performance Royalties. Priority Records on the other hand, kept 20% of the Performance Royalties and still had to pay for promotion and take care of sales. This in my opinion is one of the sweetest deals any artist ever received. Master P then dropped his project-*Ice Cream Man*-in 1996 under this deal and immediately went Gold with over 500000 copies sold.

This success was just the beginning for Master P as he ventured into other businesses like clothing lines, jewelry lines, gas stations, fast food franchises, energy drinks, phone sex companies, toy making, and much more. He even had a sports agency and declared his intention to play for the NBA. He joined the Fort Wayne Fury, a team in the minor-league Continental Basketball Association. This move later earned him tryouts with the NBA's Charlotte Hornets and Toronto Raptors, greatly exceeding most expectations but mainly because of his celebrity status, did not land a spot on a permanent NBA roster (He played pre season games for the

Hornets). In all of this, Master P maintained an independent status within the music/entertainment industry. He was one of the first figures in Hip-Hop (and potentially music in general) to achieve high levels of mainstream success without signing traditional recording contracts.

In explaining his business model, Master P said: "You spread out because you never know when it's going to end. Business is like a seesaw going up and down. When one goes down, I have the other one going up. You have to think like that if you want to survive."

Takeaway from the Master P Story

- Master P's role in shaping the current Music Business needs to be emphasized more. Before him, many artists took whatever deal the label gave them, but he changed the Music landscape to ensure that Hip-Hop artists got paid as much as other Artists.

- For an independent artist, **diversity is key**. Even though most artists are "true artists", it is possible to invest in other things so you can always stay afloat. If your albums are doing bad, you could always turn to other investments (Clothing lines, real estate, and even stocks)

- Independent **Artists must know their worth and be honest about** it. If you are good with it, do not let anybody underpay you. Any deal you sign must be reflective of your value and the amount of work you have put in as an artist, if not, stay independent.

- As a follow up to the above, there are certain deals that are not the best, but you might need those deals to propel your career to the next level. **Have the discernment** to take advantage of such deals but always have an exit strategy. Talk to a lawyer about it.

- Independent Artist must have at least a slight understanding of how the Music Business works. This puts them in a **great negotiating position** because they know exactly what they want out of the deal.

- If you must sign a deal as an independent artist, it is preferable to **sign a Distribution Deal** and not a full-blown record deal. With a distribution deal, you are in charge of your production which gives you a greater chance of controlling your masters and all you need from a label is for them to help you reach your target population and have your CDs in the places where your fans can access.

- Most importantly, **always have a LAWYER** on call to go over things with you. Master P spent $25,000 for a lawyer to negotiate one deal, but that deal set him up for the rest of life.

PART THREE

BOOKKEEPING AND TAXES FOR

SMALL BUSINESSES

This section is one of the **most important** sections of this book. Independent artists and small business owners fear taxes and often get into trouble with the IRS because they do not keep all records of their transactions. Wesley Snipes, Chris Tucker and other Hollywood big names have had issues with the IRS that resulted in (or almost resulted in) jail time. These records may also come in handy in the event of a law suit.

Benjamin Franklin once said, *"In this world, nothing can be said to be certain, except death and taxes".*

There are financial and tax implications to every business decision. That is why it is important to know the basics of taxation, but most importantly, **to seek the counsel of lawyers, financial advisors, accountants, and tax specialists.**

BOOKKEEPING FOR SMALL BUSINESSES

What is Bookkeeping?

Bookkeeping is the proper **preservation and recording of all financial affairs** of your business. To properly manage any business, we need proper bookkeeping.

Bookkeeping is particularly **important for tax purposes**. There are apps like *QuickBooks* that can help you organize your records, but you still have to understand exactly what to input.

Things that must appear in your records include:

- **Employees**

You should have records of all employees as this can change your tax responsibilities. Employers must maintain employee forms such as the **W-4 (Withholding Allowance Certification)** and **the I-9 (Employment Eligibility Verification)**.

- **Account Receivables and Payables**

This is simply a record of **what customers owe you and what you owe suppliers**. Always sign paperwork with dates, letterheads, and have the other party sign too.

- **Revenue and Expense**

A record of all money **coming in and going out**, as well as their sources and uses. It is advisable to have a business bank account and do all transactions through the bank. This way, it is easy to keep track of finances and at same time build business credit with the bank.

- **Inventory**

A record of all items, **including tangible property, Intellectual Property, and stock**. i.e. all that constitutes the business.

- **Cash**

It is important to **keep track of all the cash** that you use in your business. This can assist with accountability and make future expenditure predictions easy.

 **TheStreetlawyer's TidBit:**

At the beginning of your business venture, not all these records will be necessary. You will be dealing mostly with **limited cash, limited inventory, and few customers**; hence, it will be easy to handle your books. As the business grows, you will need the **help of tax professionals, accountants and lawyers**.

- **BUSINESS TAXES**

For entrepreneurs new to the business world, a common setback is the fear of the IRS. Thriving artists always have questions about their taxes and what to do about them.

What then are taxes?

Taxes are amounts paid to the government by individuals and businesses, to cover certain government services.

*Taxes are established on the three main principles of **fairness, efficiency** (easy to collect) and **simplicity** (easy to understand by both the tax payer and collector).

*The **three types** of taxes are:

-*Proportional Taxes* which impose the same amount on everyone, regardless of income.

-*Progressive taxes* on the other hand impose higher amounts to people with higher incomes.

-*Regressive taxes* levy greater amounts on the lower income holders.

Why Should I file my tax returns?

- The most important reason to file returns for a business owner, is **to claim adjustments against past losses**. These losses may be speculative or non-speculative in nature. These losses are reissued to the individuals and businesses in the form of tax refund checks.

- **Banks, Landlords, and Credit Card companies** may need to see **your past tax returns** before going in to business with you.

- People or businesses within a **certain tax bracket** must file returns at the end of the tax year.

- Filing returns is a sign that a **business owner is responsible**. A great track record will help when going in to subsequent transactions with other partners.

- **YOU MAY GO TO JAIL** IF YOU DO NOT FILE OR TRY TO DEFRAUD THE IRS. (They are serious about their bread)

- If you are running a business but work for another employer too, it is important to **file your taxes to claim your federal withholdings.**

SMALL BUSINESS TAX GUIDE

(Forms, Rates, Filing info)

For the purpose of this tax guide, a small business will include sole proprietors and single member LLCs.

-Small Businesses calculate their profits and losses and file it alongside their **Personal Tax Returns.**

-**Personal Returns** are filed on a **Form 1040,** while **small businesses** file their returns on a **Schedule C.**

-Because Small Businesses file their personal returns alongside their business returns **(1040+Schedule C),** the due date for filing is the same as that of personal income tax returns, which is **April 15th of each year.**

-Small businesses **must pay self-employment taxes** at the rate of **15.3% on the first $128,400** for net income and an additional **2.9% on the net income in excess** to that amount.

The table below further illustrates the different entities, tax forms, and deadlines.

Business Entity	Tax Form	Deadline to file
Sole Proprietor	-Personal return on **Form1040** -Plus **Schedule C** (Profit or Loss for a Small Business)	April 15th
Partnership (two or more partners)	Partnership files an Information Tax Return on **Form1065**. -Partners get **Schedule K-1**(individual partners profits and losses) -Individual Partners file Form 1040 alongside Schedule K-1	March 15th
LLC (Not recognized for IRS purposes)	-Single member LLC pay taxes as Sole Proprietor -Multiple member LLC pay as partnership.	April 15th or March 15th

PAYING YOUR BUSINESS TAXES

Employees earn income in form of wages. Employers **withhold a fraction of an employee's income, social security, and Medicare taxes** to forward to the IRS quarterly or monthly. This is how individuals pay their taxes and can get back refunds from their withholdings.

-As an Independent Artist, small business, or if you are self-employed, taxes cannot be withheld from your earnings.

- Sole proprietors, partners, and members of LLC are **self-employed** for IRS purposes and must therefore make Estimated Tax Payments.

-**Estimated taxes** are paid in four quarterly installments to the IRS.

-You must make the estimated tax payments if you know you are going to owe more than $1000 in federal tax for the year.

-If you **earn royalties** within any year, they should be filed as **income** on your tax return, but **if you pay for a license,** they should go as an **expenditure.**

 **TheStreetLawyer's TidBit**

If you decide to go into a joint venture with your spouse and you are joint owners of a partnership, you may qualify for a special filing case. A **qualified joint venture** will enable both partners file **Two Schedule C** forms for each person's share of the business. It is complicated. Consult with a specialist before going through.

-Also, your **choice of entity has exceeding ramification on your taxes**. Always try to pick the simplest form and seek help with taxes from jump.

PART THREE
BONUS MATERIAL

- The Billboard Charts
- Singles vs EP vs LP/Album vs Mixtape vs Cover
- 360 Degree Deals

Getting On the Billboard Charts

The Billboard Chart is the **Championship title of the Music Industry**. Those whose songs get on the chart are like teams that make it to the playoffs. I was conflicted about including this section in the book. However, I realized that some Independent Artists have **ambitions and capabilities** that transcend their various neighborhoods and city boundaries. My friend, *Anokhi the One* (Houston recording Artist and serial entrepreneur) asked me questions about this and made me realize there are Independent artists such as her who have bigger plans for their music. If your project is good enough, I would advise independent artists to think about organizing a billboard campaign.

The Billboard evaluates the weekly performances of songs and albums in the United States and other countries. According to the Billboard website, Billboard charts are based on fan interaction with an artist's music.

The metrics used to measure these fan interactions with an artist's music include:

-album sales and downloads,

-track downloads,

-radio airplay and touring as well as

-streaming and

-social interactions on Facebook, Twitter, Vevo, YouTube, Spotify and other popular online destinations for music.

Weekly **sales** and **streams charts** are monitored on a **Friday-to-Thursday cycle**. Radio **airplay song charts** however follows the **Monday to Sunday cycle**. The charts are released each Tuesday with an issue date the following Saturday, four days later.

Because Streams and sales are considered when determining a song's position on the billboard, Independent artists who do not have a single radio play can also make it to the Billboard **with an effective campaign.**

- **How Charting Works**

*Airplay is tracked through **Broadcast Data System (BDS)**. BDS uses digital pattern-recognition technology to identify songs that air on radio and TV channels across the United States and Canada. **This process is done 24/7 and captures over 100 million songs annually.**

The data from BDS is used not only by Billboard, but also by radio stations, record company executives, publishing firms, performance rights organizations, music retailers, and film and TV producers.

*Billboard takes **social media** and **streaming** into consideration now. It was not until 2005 that streaming became popular. It took a few more years for the first nontraditional artist to make their way to the Billboard Top 100 Charts. In **2012, Dj Baauer's Harlem Shake** was released on YouTube, and it stayed on the Billboard 100 for over five weeks. Artists must engage with their fans though the comment sections of social media platforms, they must also encourage fans to mention their music. Getting fans to hashtag albums or singles is an effective way to increase sales and therefore get a place on the charts.

* **Album sales** is the biggest consideration in getting charted. The Billboard uses the **Nielsen SoundScan** which tracks sales of music and music videos in the US and Canada. Independent artists need to get a **UPC (Universal Product Codes) code** for their albums. These are 12-digit numbers attached to your project which makes it recognizable and traceable throughout the world. If you go through CDbaby or Distrokid, you are assigned a UPC code for your products, but you can also get an individual code online. By scanning a UPC code, the system collects sales information from about 14,000 retail and nontraditional sources like online stores and concert sales.

 **TheStreetLawyer's TidBit**

- For an independent artist to be assured of a position on the billboard, they need to sell between **450 to 500 albums in the first week**. This is an easy number for major labels, since they own distribution channels and have aggressive marketing plans. An independent artist can do the same by organizing a serious **"pre-order campaign"** for your album. All sales prior to the actual release date **are counted as Week One Sales**.

- It is important to **promote your project**. Enough noise should be made amongst your supporters in anticipation of your release. Remind them that the project is on the way and when its done, let them know too. Come up with creative ways to do this; increase tours and performances to get new fans and be in touch with old fans.

- **Sell it cheap.** If your project is affordable, many more people will buy it. You do not have to cheat yourself, but making a song affordable may result in an increase demand which will lead to quick turnovers and in turn increase sales and profits.

- **Release several versions** of your song. All the various versions of your song (covers, acapella, chop n screw etc.) will be counted as the same song for charting purposes. Different people will like different versions, so put out every version you feel inspired to and it will increase your chances of landing a spot in the *Music Playoffs Chart.*

- **Get some radio attention.** It is difficult for an Indie Artist to have the connections to the top radio stations, but it could be easy for them to contact college radio stations and online radio channels who can easily play their song. If it is a good project, more radios will pick it up.

SINGLES vs EP vs LP vs ALBUM vs MIXTAPE vs COVER

These are about the most confusing terms in Music Industry Lingo. It is important for independent artists to know the differences between these terms. An understanding of what these various terms are, and if aptly applied could lead to massive success with projects. These are all bodies of work which vary according to format and length.

Singles are recordings (usually 1-3 tracks) **under ten minutes of play**. In most cases, a single is released for promotional purposes before an album drops. The singles released are usually the best songs of the project that could lead more people to buy the project when it is finally released. In the current climate, Singles have come to stand for **one track**. There are artists in this day and time who do nothing but drop singles alongside their videos. This is a release strategy that could be very helpful to independent artists as they can release singles daily, giving their fans a chance to enjoy their content while at the same time giving them the chance to get better at their art. iTunes stores and Spotify accept as many as three tracks less than ten minutes each as a single.

An **Extended Play (EP)** on the other hand is a body of work which is too long to be a single, but too short to be an album. A typical EP has **3-6 songs** with a playtime of not more than **30mins**. There are some EPs that are way longer than thirty minutes, but thirty is the accepted time. An EP might be a shorter version of an album, sold for promotional purposes and in preparation for the release of the album. This is an important tool for independent artist as it could prove pivotal in breaking in to the industry.

Long Play (LP) otherwise called **Album** is usually **longer than six songs** and there is no limit to how many tracks could be on an album. An album is supposed to be a complete experience from the artist to the fans. **Lyrical content, production, mixing& mastering, album covers are just a few of the things that an album is judged on.** Artists should take out the time to promote projects before dropping them. The organization, flow of tracks, overall message of the album and how each individual single furthers or contrast this message are all things to be considered when selecting songs for an album. As mentioned above, Singles and EPs could be released earlier to promote the album. These are the easiest projects to make it to the Charts

Mixtapes on the other hand are a compilation of work put together mostly for promotional reasons. There is an increasing trend of artists using original beats and still calling their projects mixtapes. **In the past, mixtapes were mostly upcoming artists rapping on other people's beats**, or seasoned artists going in on the hottest new beats so their fans could have something to listen to while waiting on their original projects. **Mixtapes are rarely ever sold** (except physical copies, to upset cost of production) and because they are for free, an artist will not have to pay for sample clearances when they used another's beat.

Covers are a different ball game. The *Chicago Tribune* described the term [cover] in 1952: "*trade jargon meaning to record a tune that looks like a potential hit on someone else's label*". After the **Copyright Act of 1909**, musicians in the US have had the right to record a version of another artist's **recorded and released tune**. A license can be negotiated with the owner of the original recordings, or the artist could get a compulsory mechanical license through the Harry Fox Agency. This license is cheap and gives you the right to do a rendition of the original song which you can sell.

- **360 Degree Deals**

Under a traditional record deal, the artist only gave the record label **the right to share in the income from their artist's record sales.** The artists still controlled other revenue sources like **touring, merchandising and publishing.** The advent of streaming drastically reduced profitability for the record labels **who desired to increase profitability by managing everything for the artist- hence a 360 deal.** Under this type of recording contract, record labels retain complete control over an artist's **publishing rights, touring rights,** as well as **merchandising rights.**

The artists controlled certain rights under the traditional deal which included decision-making in:

-booking and choosing tours

-contracting with third parties

-branding and merchandising

-artists development

An artist who signs **a 360-degree deal gives up control of every aspect of their career.** This is not necessarily a bad thing because some artists find it overwhelming to handle every aspect of their careers. Cardi B just signed a 360 deal and hopefully, it will work perfect for her. **However, most label owners are vultures, looking for the next best thing**. This could lead them to "shelf" certain artists while promoting others who bring them more money.

The new Music Industry has evolved in such a way that it is less overwhelming to keep up with various aspects of an artist career. In the digital age, aspects of an artist careers can be **outsourced** to different organization, but the artist still has control.

TheStreetLawyer's TidBit

- Independent Artists should be looking for **Distribution Deals** and not complete record deals. If you control your production, you don't have to share 50% of your masters with outside producers. You could negotiate a fairer rate within your team.

- It is difficult as an independent artist to organize large tours. However, **getting a good booking agent** on your team will help. Most of them are highly connected within the industry and can take your career to heights.

- Companies such **as distrokid, CD Baby, and TuneCore, assist artists in distribution and collection of royalties**. A one-time flat fee registration will cover you for a whole year.

- If you are a creative, you will likely be surrounded by other creatives. **Get a street team** to help you in the designing and sales of merchandize.

- By all means, keep **working on yourself and your art**.

- Note that if you sign a record deal and are given an **advancement**, this money comes from your share of the income. **Advancements are not free money**. It is like an artist taking an early loan from his paycheck (I know you know a thing or two about payday loans). Once your project drops and starts bringing in income, the record label then must **recoup (recoupment)** this amount before you are given the rest of your money. If the advancement amount is more than the gross income from your project (meaning you had a bad project which did not sell) then the artist ends up **owing the Record Label.**

PART FOUR

BASIC CONTRACT LAW

Most artists are "true artists". They prefer to concentrate on their craft—and hardly have time to look at blueprints. Hence, booming careers are cut short, and musician royalties are stolen by industry vultures.

The music industry is mostly governed by the law of contracts. Contractual relationships include record labels extending record deals to up-and-coming artists, artists recruiting producers, companies extending endorsement deals to popping artists and artists recruiting management teams and booking agents. There is an unending list of these relationships in the music business.

Independent artists and record labels, especially in the early stages, when they are unable to hire a legal team, are charged with the responsibility of understanding the basic principles and terms of agreements they make.

They must understand what a contract is, how a contract is created, the terms of a contract, termination of a contract, and the most important contracts in the music business.

Not knowing the basics of any contract you sign, or the parties involved, can turn your passion in to your worst nightmare.

- **WHAT IS A CONTRACT**

A contract is an agreement or promise that a **court of law** is willing **to enforce**.

Contracts can be **written or oral**. In years long gone, a "gentleman's handshake" was all you needed to establish a contractual relationship, but today it is advisable to have the terms down in writing and signed by both parties because in this day and age, *people really be fake.*

The court **does not enforce all agreements** between parties. If a record label owner promises to give you studio time on Friday and later refuses, the courts will be reluctant to punish the label owner. The artist did not give anything of value in exchange for this promise. Maybe your aunt told you to give up on your music career for five million dollars when you graduate college. Upon graduation, she refuses to pay you, but you gave up your music career. You can then turn to the courts to enforce this agreement.

- **ENFORCEABLE CONTRACTS**

As mentioned earlier, not all agreements are enforceable by the courts. Agreements that are within the court's power to enforce must contain:

a) **An Offer**

b) **Acceptance of the Offer**

c) **Consideration**

d) **No Valid Defenses**

OFFER + Acceptance + Consideration + NO Valid Defenses = ENFORCEABLE CONTRACT

OFFER

OFFER + Acceptance + Consideration + NO Valid Defenses = ENFORCEABLE CONTRACT

An offer is a purposeful display of a present intent to enter into an agreement with another party.

This purposeful display of present intent can be **demonstrated** by a **promise, commitment, or undertaking** made to the other party.

An offer must have **clear** and **definite** terms. It must give the other party the power to accept.

Ex: **I want to sign you to my label for an advance of $5000.** This is an offer because it shows the label owner's present willingness to sign the artist for $5000, if the artist agrees.

If any reasonable person would infer from another's words that they intended to make a contract, then the courts will recognize an offer.

Price quotes, rewards, and auctions do not constitute offers since their terms are neither clear nor definite and they do not give the power to the other party to accept and close the deal.

An offer can be **terminated** through **lapse of time** (where the other party fails to accept the offer within specified or reasonable period), **death or incapacity** of either party, and by **rejection** (where the other party does not agree to the current terms of offer).

ACCEPTANCE

Offer + **ACCEPTANCE** + Consideration + NO Valid Defenses = ENFORCEABLE CONTRACT

The second thing that must be present in an enforceable contract is acceptance. Acceptance is the purposeful display of agreement to the terms of the offer in a manner **invited** or **required** by the offer.

Acceptance must mirror the terms of the offer. Major changes to the subject matter of the contract will not count as acceptance but as a **counter-offer**.

Ex: Janky Pro offers to buy Demante's old recorder for $75. This is an offer. For Demante to accept this offer, all he must do is say yes and take the $75 from Janky Pro. However, if Demante decides that he wants to sell the merchandise for $100 instead, this becomes a major change and will not be an acceptance anymore. It will mean Demante **rejected** that offer and made a **counter-offer**.

The person making the offer is the **King/Queen of the deal** and can determine the **manner of acceptance**. If he/she fails to do so, acceptance can be made in any **reasonable manner**. In the industry, it will mostly require you to read through paperwork, and if you agree, you sign it.

Silence does not equal acceptance: except when the other party benefits from the subject of the offer, the party has reason to know the offer could be accepted by silence, or because of **previous dealings**, it is reasonable that the receiving party **communicates their rejection** of the offer.

CONSIDERATION

Offer + Acceptance + **CONSIDERATION+** NO Valid Defenses = ENFORCEABLE CONTRACT

This is the **value that is paid in exchange** for the promise. If a songwriter wants a producer to work on their song, and the producer charges $100/hr., the consideration will be the $100 paid in exchange for the production services.

Consideration **must be sufficient**. Anything of legal value is sufficient consideration. This will include money or a promise **to do or refrain** from doing something.

Consideration **must also be adequate,** meaning the things exchanged must have some approximate value. Ten dollars for a car, though sufficient, is inadequate.

NO VALID DEFENSE

Offer + Acceptance + Consideration + **NO VALID DEFENSE** = ENFORCEABLE CONTRACT

This is the fourth and final component of an enforceable contract. Sometimes, an offer, acceptance, and consideration are present but there exists a reason the court will **excuse performance from one party or both.** The absence of any valid defense means that we have an enforceable contract, but **the presence of a valid defense means that even though there is contract, the law will not recognize it** in certain circumstances.

Examples of valid defenses include:

- **Misrepresentation**

This is a false assertion of fact. Misrepresentation could be Negligent, Fraudulent or Innocent.

- **Nondisclosure/Concealment**

This is a **positive action** done with the intention of preventing another from learning the facts. The nondisclosure **must be material**, and there must be reliance on the non-disclosure.

- **Mistake**

This is a belief that is not in accord with facts. It could be **unilateral** (Only one party misinterprets the meaning of essential terms) or **bilateral** (both parties misinterpret essential terms to the contract.

- **Duress**

Duress is using **any kind of force** to get one party to agree to the terms of a contract. This could be **physical duress, unlawful threat, or economic duress.**

- **Undue Influence**

This is the **unfair power** one party has over another or where the receiving party, based only on their relationship, is justified in thinking that the other party cannot act against their welfare.

- **Public Policy**

This may be raised as a defense especially where the subject matter of the contract is illegal.

Ex. Prostitution Contract, or contract to kill.

- **Incapacity**

It invalidates a contract. Incapacity will include infancy, mental incapacity, or temporal incapacity (temporal drunkenness).

- **Unconscionability**

If a contract is **so unfair that no reasonable person will ask for it**, then it could be used as a defense to contract formation. For example, **Adhesion contracts and certain non-compete agreements.**

- **Statute of Frauds**

Even though we mentioned earlier that contracts do not necessarily need to be written, **certain contracts must be written** or else they will not be enforced by the courts. These include:

-contracts for **marriage**,

-contracts that will **not be completed within 1 year** of formation (note),

-contracts for **sale of land**,

-contract for an **executor**,

-contract for **suretyship**, and

-contracts for sale of **goods over $500**.

Apart from these valid defenses, a party can be **excused from performance** if a **condition** to his performance has not been met. If it is **impossible or impracticable** for party to perform, or if performance will no longer serve the purpose of the contract (**frustration of purpose**), a party can be excused as well.

 **TheStreetLawyer's TidBit**

Every time you sign a contract or when you prepare one, please go through this list of defenses. Some of the defenses, if successfully used, **destroy the contract**. The party who successfully pleads any of these defenses has the option to go ahead with the contract or back out.

Parties to a contract could also request **a cure i.e. fixing the contract**, rather than completely abandoning every aspect of it. Be sure to consult with a lawyer for more help.

OTHER IMPORTANT CONCEPTS IN CONTRACT LAW

- **BREACH**

A breach occurs where one party to the contract **fails to perform services** as agreed in the contract terms. After both parties have agreed to the terms, each party must fulfill their obligations. Failure to do so, for whatever reason will be a breach.

A breach is **material if it seriously affects the subject of the contract**. In such a case, the non-breaching party is excused from his performance and can still sue for **damages**.

An **immaterial breach** on the other hand, does not greatly affect the other party's performance as the breaching party has substantially performed already. Here the non-breaching party is **entitled to damages**, but his **obligations are not suspended.**

Substantial performance is when the breaching party performs all aspects of the contract except for minor deviations. The **breaching party is still entitled to payment** under the contract but **minus the damages** suffered by the incomplete performance.

The party who has substantially performed is still entitled **in fairness the right to complete their performance even after the breach**. This is known as **cure**. After the breaching party "cures" his wrong, he may still be liable to pay damages for the breach which will of course be way less than if he had straight out breached.

- **THIRD PARTY BENEFICIARIES (TPB)**

A contract confers right only to the parties involved. Only the parties to this contract can sue to enforce it. However, **in rare exceptions** where the contract involves **third party beneficiaries** (TPB), or the contract rights and **duties are transferred to third parties**, other parties not directly involved in the contract can sue to enforce it.

TPB are not parties to the contract, they just benefit from the contract. They could either be intended or incidental TPB.

Intended TPB are either designated in the contract, directly benefits from the contract, or has some relationship with one of the contracting parties such that it can be inferred they are an intended beneficiary. An **Incidental Beneficiary** does not meet any of the above but still benefits from the contract.

For Example: Cameron Jovi, contracts with Construction Inc. to fix the road leading up to Tzy Panchack's home and Panchack is roommates with Mr. Leo. Jovi and Construction Inc. are parties to the contract, Panchack is the **intended TPB** and Mr. Leo is the **Incidental TPB**.

Intended TPB can sue to enforce the contract but only the principal parties can modify the contract. So Panchack has no right to tell Construction Inc. which road to do, but he can sue to have them finish their work. Mr. Leo on the other hand can benefit from the road but cannot sue to enforce compliance by Construction Inc.

Assignments and Delegations involve third parties in a contract. **An Assignment** is the transfer of a RIGHT to a third party **after** a contract has been formed. All rights can be assigned except those that will materially change the duties of whoever has to perform. **Delegations** occur when a party to a contract transfers his DUTIES to a third party after formation. All duties can be delegated **except with personal services**, or when the contract terms expressly prohibit delegation.

- **DAMAGES**

If a party suffers a breach in a contract, they can sue the other party. If the court agrees that there was an enforceable contract whose terms were in fact breached, the court can award damages. These damages make up for loss that has been suffered by the party. The court could award **money damages** or **equitable remedies**.

Money damages are computed to cover a person's **expectation interest** (puts party in condition he would have been if the other party performed i.e. Harm Suffered-Savings Realized); **reliance interest** (puts non-breaching party in position he was before contract was made); or **restitution interest** (here breaching party pays back the exact amount owed).

Equitable Remedies exists to cloth the naked bones of the law. The law is blind, and this blindness may have several positive aspects, but it comes with some flaws too. **Equity uses principles of fairness where money damages will not suffice**. The most common equitable remedies include **specific performance** (court forces party to perform a particular action) and **injunctions** (court forces party to refrain from acting a certain way).

Parties could also come up with **agreed-to-remedies.** Here both parties agree to what damages will be paid in an event of a breach. **The Liquidated Damages clause** in your home rental application is an example of this.

D. OTHER FORMS OF "CONTRACTUAL" RELATIONSHIPS

We earlier defined a contract as "a set of promises that the court is willing to enforce". For a promise to climb up to the level of a contract, certain elements (offer, acceptance, consideration, and lack of a valid defense) must be present. However, there are certain relationships that may not rise to the level of a contract, **but the court will still be willing and able to intervene under equity**.

Fiduciary Relationship

A fiduciary relationship is one in which one party undertakes to take care of the **money and/or assets of another** (entrustor/principal). Usually, one party has the technical knowledge which the other party lacks. The courts are interested in making sure that the owner of the assets or money does not get swindled by the fiduciary, **who usually has more knowledge in the field and is overall more sophisticated.**

Lord Millett in <u>Bristol and West Building Society v Mothew</u>" defines a fiduciary as:

"someone who has undertaken to act for and on behalf of another in a particular matter in circumstances which give rise to a relationship of trust and confidence."

The fiduciary **must always act solely in the interest of the entrustor/principal**. The fiduciary has two main duties owed to the entrustor- a duty of care, and a duty of loyalty.

The Duty of Care requires the fiduciary to **make decisions in good faith and after reasonable research** on behalf of the principal. Fiduciaries must take all available information in to account and then act in a manner that protects the interest of the principal. Fiduciaries should never seek self-gains. Duty of care can be summed up in the requirement that **a fiduciary/manager should be present, informed, engaged, use good and independent judgment, utilize expert advice and trusted information, refer to meeting minutes, and seek to stay abreast of legal developments, good governance, and best practices within the industry**.

The Duty of Loyalty always requires the fiduciary to be completely loyal to the principal. The fiduciary must act in the **best interest of the entrustor/principal and avoid all conflict of interest**. This duty requires fiduciaries to keep confidential, and not disclose or use, any information that they come across in their official capacity as fiduciaries. They must **report all conflicts of interest**, whether actual or potential, real or perceived, and obtain legal advice in cases where it is unclear whether or not a conflict exists.

Examples of Fiduciary Relationships

- **Principal/Agent:** Under a principal/agent relationship, an agent is appointed to act on behalf of the principal without conflict of interest. An example of this is Companies appointing a board to act on its behalf. The assets of the business belong to the company, but the Board or the shareholders are appointed as agents to oversee these assets

- **Attorney/Client:** Attorneys must always act in **complete fairness to their clients**. Trust and confidence must exist between the client and attorney. Attorneys are held liable for breaches of their fiduciary duties by the client and are accountable to the court in which that client is represented when a breach occurs.

- **Manager/Record label/artists:** A special fiduciary relationship exists **between labels, managers, and artists**. An artist must be able to trust and rely on information given by management or the record label. Hence the courts **will be more than willing to**

impose a fiduciary duty on managers to use due diligence and care in dealing with the assets and career of the artist. Certain wrongs that may not rise to the level of a breach of contract, may very well be recognized as a breach of fiduciary duty.

Breaches in Fiduciary Duty in the Music Industry

A breach of fiduciary duty happens when a fiduciary relationship is in place and actions are taken by the fiduciary, which are contrary to the interest of the entrustor or principal. In the music industry, this will mostly take the form of **Managers or record labels, misrepresenting the terms of a contract, or not fully disclosing information about the contract.** This could also take the form of **misappropriation of artist funds.** For certain wrongs, an artist might not be able to prevail under a breach of contract claim but could very well find a solution in a **breach of fiduciary duty claim.**

To prevail in a breach of fiduciary duty tort claim, a plaintiff must show that there was

- **a duty owed by the fiduciary**: This can be easily proven if there was a written contract establishing a relationship

- **a breach of that duty**: this can be established by providing facts and evidence that show that a manager failed to disclose important information, neglected his responsibilities, misappropriated funds, or misrepresented certain facts.

- **Damages:** A plaintiff must show that he suffered **actual damages** to prevail in this claim. The damages do not have to be large. As long as you suffered some kind of damage, and the court can find that the actions of the fiduciary were **fraudulent and malicious**, you can also earn punitive damages, consequential damages, attorney fees and court cost.

PART FOUR BONUS MATERIAL

Every Business must have an exit plan. In technology for example, you either go public and sell shares to investors (Facebook), or you build the company and sell it to another rival (WhatsApp). Independent artists, much like any business, must plan on how to transcend that initial success. They can either sign a record deal or run their own label. Either way, they will need to understand:

- **Personnel in the music Industry,**
- **Their roles, and**
  - **Typical industry contracts.**

Table: **Personnel in the Music Industry**

TITLE	ROLE
ARTIST MANAGER	POOR SOUL! The manger takes all the heat. "A good manager acts as a shield for artists so they can bare their soul," Marie Trout. The manager acts as a liaison between artists and other industry personnel. His main duties involve: organizing band practices or studio sessions, managing the finances, putting out "fires", organizing tours, handling everyday business. He is the glue that holds the unit together.
BOOKING AGENT	AT the early stage of your career, this role is played by the manager or the independent artist. The booking agent secures shows, bargains fee arrangements, organizes tours, and club appearances. They take a percentage of the live shows an artist does.
RADIO PLUG	There are those Socialites in the city that know every DJ; they hang out with the who is who. These are mostly Party promoters who spend time building relationships in the industry so if they give your songs to the radio Djs, it is likely to get some airtime. Every artist needs this kind of plug. I know we are in the internet age of Music but do not underestimate the power of radio promotions.
ENTERTAINMENT ATTORNEY	As my friend Denise Gregory Esq. says, "Paperwork makes the paper work" Very early in any artist career, it is necessary to have some form of legal representation. There are many young lawyers building their entertainment practices who will be willing to build with you for little or no fees. Entertainment attorneys draft contracts, prepare paperwork, secure permits, negotiate and read over contracts. They also protect your Intellectual Property (Registering Trademarks, negotiating license agreements, negotiating endorsement deals, and securing copyrights and the royalties.
ACCOUNTANT	It is necessary to have a "numbers guy". Get an ambitious young Certified Public Accountant (CPA) "straight outta school" and build with them. The accountant alongside your attorney should advise you on your taxes, file your taxes, take care of your books and make sure all your accounts are balanced.

SHOW PROMOTERS/ STREET TEAM	Show Promoters/Street team play a major role in the career of an independent artists. They help put people on your music, merchandize and your team. They attend events and promote your overall brand, they rep your merchandize and get your social media popping. Family and close friends make the best promoters and street team.
EXECUTIVE PRODUCER	This is the person who finances the project. He also owns the rights to the Master recording. For independent labels, signing an artist gives you rights to these master recordings in exchange for the fee you pay them, hence the executive producer should be from the label. For independent Artist, it is good to save up and be your executive producer, that way you own all your rights. But if have that money-friend, make them your Executive producer.(FreeGame)
PRODUCER (MUSIC)	Mostly a musician or audio engineer. They supervise the creative aspects of recording a project. Independent labels need a few individuals with that good creative ear who can structure a song, adding flavors that makes the song or project better. It is advisable to pay them upfront and a one-time lumpsum for any project, that way they do not have any rights to an artist's royalties. These are the guys that own studios and know how to play around with fruity loop studio.
A&R PERSON	The "Artists and Repertoire" Person applies mostly to independent labels than artists. He is a scout who discovers up and coming talent, gets the label to sign him, and strategically works to push the artist's brand. Independent label owners can play this role.

The New Music Business model offers a chance for an Independent Artist to play all these roles. However, it is important to seek help with the technical issues. Focus on your art, and get experts to monetize your art.

LIST OF CONTRACTS

Below is a list of Contracts every Independent Artist should be aware of and every Independent Record Label should have. Please consult with an attorney or slide in my DM about drafting and negotiating these contracts as boiler plate/ "internet" contracts may not completely represent your agreement.

NAME	COMPONENTS
TRANSFER OF RIGHTS CONTRACT	Independent Artist are constantly collaborating with other artists. Whilst this is very advisable, it leads to unnecessary problem especially when a collaboration does really good. It is important to have "Transfer of rights" contract for every collaboration
	The essential terms of this contract should include: i) distribution of income (royalties) ii) performance rights iii) ownership rights.
RECORD DEAL / ARTIST CONTRACTS	Record deals typically cover a song or project that an artist does, and a label is interested in. The label buys the masters to the song or project. This should be distinguished from artists contracts that cover multiple projects and have a longer term.
	The essential terms of a Record deal/ Artist Contract are: i) production volume ii) format iii) exclusivity iv) duration v) sub-license rights vi) sync and merchandising rights.
DISTRIBUTION CONTRACTS	Every Independent Artist should try to get a distribution deal. Distributors know the market and have way more connections. They can put your music in front of many fans. Independent artists do not need to sell their master rights, they can negotiate for a percentage of the sales or pay an upfront fee.
	The essential terms of a distribution deal are: i) distribution are ii) recordings covered by contract iii) protective rights and stock management iv) release v) cost and payment transaction with collection societies
ARTIST MANAGEMENT CONTRACTS	The manager works alongside the booking agent and they must both have contracts. They are charged with representing the interest of the artist
	Essential terms for management and booking agent contracts include: i) Power of attorney ii) limitation of representation only to business matter iii) duties iv) Compensation v) Duration of representation vi) conflict of interest.

GUEST PERFORMANCE CONTRACTS	These contracts should be signed between booking agents, promoters, clubs and every place where the artists take their talent. Essential Terms of a Guest performance contract include: i) location, date, length and time ii) duties of artist and promoters iii) fee and type of payment iv) cancellation agreement and related fees v) insurance vi) Collection Society Contributions
PRODUCER CONTRACTS	Labels usually hire producers to work on artist projects. The main thing is determining if this producer gets paid a one-time fee or there is a split-arrangement on the royalties. Producer sometime sign an independent artist, develop him and get him signed by a major label. Producer contracts should include: i) fee sharing agreements, ii) hire status (employee or independent contractor) iii) duties iv) length of agreement

There are many more contracts you may need that have not been mentioned here, however these are the basics to get your endeavor running. The terms mentioned here are just the most essential, other terms may be relevant in different situations. Make sure to consult with a lawyer who will help with your individualized needs.

EPILOGUE

COGNITION FOR INDEPENDENT ARTISTS

The new Music Business demands a plethora of talents from independent artists. They must have basic proficiency in contract law, taxation, bookkeeping, intellectual property, business management and marketing amongst other disciplines. Therefore, independent artists must be able to learn a multitude of things and they must be able to learn them **really fast**. When asked about the secret behind his viral hit Old Town Road, Atlanta Country/ Rap star Lil Nas X said he simply made fifty memes and used the song in the background, some of those memes went viral, and so did the song. The *"Contrapper"* (you heard it here first), is very social media savvy, he also can play the trumpet, and he can lay down a good mélange of hip hop and country music. How was he and other high achievers able to gain all these skills? The answer lies in Cognitive Psychology.

What is Cognitive Psychology?

The Miriam Webster Online medical Dictionary defines Cognitive psychology as "a branch of psychology concerned with mental processes (as perception, thinking, learning, and memory)". It deals with **how we learn and store information.**

School teaches us what to study, but there is not enough emphasis on how to retain and use that information. In learning any skill, an organized system will be more effective and efficient. Much of the research on the human mental process in recent years, pointed to the work of Dr K. Anders Ericsson, Professor of Psychology at Florida State University. Dr Ericsson studied experts at the top of their various fields and concluded that **the more time a person spent in deliberate practice, the better they got at that thing.** He also noted that nearly every person at the top of their career had spent at least 10,000 hours over a period of ten years practicing.

This concept of **10,000 hours** was further popularized by **Malcom Gladwell** in his best seller, *The Outlier* (a must read) in which he argues that **success is never an individual effort but the effort of a community** of interrelated factors that position certain individuals to outshine the rest. **Successful individuals to him, are those who have been afforded, and take the opportunity to deliberately repeat that skill in an organized way.** The experts he interviewed had each spent about 10,000 hours of practice.

Indie Artists **do not** need to be experts to thrive in the business, they just need to effectively organize themselves as a business which requires learning a multitude of skills. The challenge is looking for an inexpensive way to learn all the things we need to know with the limited time and resources we have,-hence the twenty-hour rule.

The "New" twenty-hour Rule

As Independent Artist, we are often thrown in the wild at the start of our careers. As J. Cole puts it, all we have is "a dollar and a dream". Looking at what the Dreamville boss has done with that "dollar and dream", there is hope for those who believe. To reinforce our believes, we need to back it with works. Independent Artists must be ready to acquire a plethora of skills which will help them in running a **profitable "business"** within this Industry. It may be that some artists have to learn to play an instrument to make their live performances more electrifying, and it may be for others that they need to pick up some knowledge on accounting. **Whatever the need, the challenge remains the scarcity of resources and time** especially for the Independent artist. How then do we acquire these skills on a "beginners' budget"?

Josh Kaufman, in his book *The first 20 hours*, (another must read) offers an answer to this question. Learning a new skill could be overwhelming but in the current economic environment, learning new skills and adapting is necessary for the survival of any startup and independent artists at the start of their careers are in fact startups. It is easy to become proficient at anything if we practice enough.

"Practice" here is defined as **the systematic and focused repetition of a skill**. But, how much practice do we need? How do we organize the material? How often do we practice? These are some of the questions that cognitive psychology seeks to answer.

Kaufman argues that all we need is **twenty hours to get proficient at any skill** i.e., twenty hours to go from knowing absolutely nothing to becoming really good. Notice that he does not say twenty hours to become an expert. As Independent Artists, we must strive for perfection, but we do not need to be at an expert level in the field to make money. Hence, it is more appropriate to focus on how to get proficient in any skill and according to Kaufman's research, all we need is twenty hours.

Kaufman breaks down the twenty hours to **forty minutes a day, spread out over a month**. He notes that the best time to practice is before bedtime as it is easier to remember the things you did immediately prior to sleep and even easier for those things to register in your subconscious. Kaufman proposes these five steps to learning any new skill in twenty hours. These are the same five steps **he used to learn the ukulele** in twenty hours.

1. Decide what you want

At this stage Kaufman insists that we must have a clear and complete goal of what we are trying to achieve. We must define what success will look like for us here.

For an Independent Artist, the goal might be learning to play a new instrument or learning how to use a recording Equipment. Once we have identified what we want to achieve, and what we want our end result to be (proficiency level) then it is time to move to the second step.

2. Deconstruct the Skill

Here Kaufman calls for a breakdown of the skill into subparts to figure out which ones are the most important sub skills that must be learned first

In learning how to play the guitar for example, deconstructing the skill will be breaking it down to the various chords, learning how to move the fingers, and how the strings work.

3. Learn Enough to Self-Correct

It is at this point that we do some deeper research. We collect 3-5 resources that can give us enough knowledge about our desired skill set. It is this knowledge that will enable us to begin actual practice.

In going through resources online for example, the themes that keep repeating themselves from the various sources, should be studied. If every resource says knowledge of chords is a great starting point to learning the guitar, it will be useful to consider the information and start from there.

4. Remove barriers

At this stage, Kaufman does not only call for the removal of anything that is a distraction but insists that we do anything that will make it easier for us to practice. We need to limit the distractions during the practice time so we can make the most of each session.

It is important to keep our material/instruments in places that remind us to practice. Having a guitar in the living room is better than keeping it on a tall shelf or dark corridor.

5. Pre-Commit to twenty hours at least

Kaufman notes here that the beginning is always rough and so it is important to pre-commit the first twenty hours.

If we repeat any skill in a focused and organized manner for at least twenty hours, we are going to be proficient in that skill. Pick that guitar, pick that piano, pick that accounting book, and as Kaufman always says, "twenty hours is all you need"!

SELECTED BIBLIOGRAPHY

Albert, Jane, 2010, House of Hits: The Great Untold Story of Australia's First Family of Music. Melbourne and London: Hardie Grant Books.

Alderman, John, 2001, Sonic Boom: Napster; MP3 and the New Pioneers of Music. London: Fourth Estate.

Allen, Paul, 2011, Artist Management for the Music Business. Amsterdam: Focal Press.

Bradley, Andy and Roger Wood, 2010, House of Hits: The Story of Houston's Gold Star/Sugarhill Recording Studios. Houston: University of Texas Press.

Bronson, Fred, 2003, The Billboard Book of Number 1 Hits. The Inside Story Behind Every Number One Single on Billboard's Hot 100 From 1955 to the Present. Updated and expanded 5th edition. New York: Billboard Books.

Brooks, Tim, 2005, Lost Sounds. Blacks and the Birth of the recording industry 1890-1919. Champaign: University of Illinois Press.

Gladwell, Malcolm, 2008-. **Outliers**: The Story of Success. New York: Little, Brown and Co.

Hughes, Diane, Guy Morrow, Sarah Keith and Mark L. Evans, 2016, The New Music Industries. Disruption and Discovery. Palgrave Macmillan/Springer.

Hull, Geoffrey P., 1998, The Recording Industry. Boston etc.: Allyn and Bacon.

Hull, Geoffrey P., Thomas Hutchison and Richard Strasser, 2010, The Music Business and Recording Industry. New York: Routledge.

Josh Kaufman, 2014, The First 20 Hours: How to Learn Anything . . . Fast!

Passman, Donald S., 2011, All You Need to Know About the Music Business, 8th edition. New York: Free Press.

Pecknold, Diane, 2007, The Selling Sound. The Rise of the Country Music Industry. Durham and London: Duke University Press.

Perry, Megan, 2008, How to be a Record Producer in the Digital Era. New York. Billboard Books.

Soames, Nicolas, 2012, The Story of Naxos: The Extraordinary Story of the Independent Record Label That Changed Classical Recording for Ever. London: Piatkus Books.

Tschmuck, Peter, Philip L. Pearce and Steven Campbell, 2013, Music Business and the Experience Economy. The Australasian Case. Heidelberg & New York: Springer (book review)

IRS Website, https://www.irs.gov/

ABOUT THE AUTHOR:

Emmanuel has always had a keen interest in Music and has played various roles in The Music Industry. During his undergraduate years at the University of Kentucky, he DJed part time which put him in contact with several big names and underground stars in the Industry.

He later moved to Charlotte, North Carolina for law school, where he focused on Entertainment and Sports Law. While in Law school, he participated in the Entrepreneurship and Community Development Clinics respectively which exposed him to the Independent Music and Small Business grind. The vibrant music scene in Charlotte pushed him to Artist Management and representation.

Emmanuel is currently building an Entertainment Law/Business Consultancy & Advisory Firm in Houston Texas which is dedicated to assisting Independent artists and record labels navigate the complexities of this New Music Industry.

He holds a BA in International Relations, a BSc in Political Science both from the University of Kentucky, Lexington, KY. He also holds a Juris Doctorate from the Charlotte School of Law and recently earned a Certificate from the World Intellectual Property Organization (WIPO) Geneva, Switzerland on Intellectual Property and the Transfer of Technology.

You Can stay connected with Emmanuel via:

Email – mackenah@gmail.com

Instagram - @thestreetlawyer_

www.ingramcontent.com/pod-product-compliance
Lightning Source LLC
Chambersburg PA
CBHW020749230426
43665CB00009B/548